HOME BUSINESS IDEAS

Innovative Ways to Quit your 9 to 5 and Create Multiple Streams of Income

Copyright © 2018. All Rights Reserved.

No part of this publication may be reproduced, distributed, or transmitted in any form or by any means, including photocopying, recording, or other electronic or mechanical methods, or by any information storage and retrieval system without the prior written permission of the publisher, except in the case of very brief quotations embodied in critical reviews and certain other noncommercial uses permitted by copyright law.

Table of Contents

Introduction 1

Chapter 1: Get Paid Writing Song Reviews 5

Chapter 2: Organize Festivals and Collect Money from Vendors 7

Chapter 3: Investing in Stocks 9

Chapter 4: Mystery Shopping 11

Chapter 5: Create a Transportation Service for the Elderly 15

Chapter 6: Laundry Service 19

Chapter 7: Online Researcher 23

Chapter 8: Start a Dog Walking Business 29

Chapter 9: Independent Travel Consultant 37

Chapter 10: Website Tester 43

Chapter 11: Sell Your T-Shirt Designs 47

Chapter 12: Transcribing Audio & Video 49

Chapter 13: Online Tutor 53

Chapter 14: Get Going! 57

Before you continue, do you want a free book that teaches you additional ways to start a successful home business?

If you answered YES, you're in the right place. The methods described in this book teach you how to efficiently run a business.

Right now, you can get a **FREE** copy of **Small Business Mastery: A Comprehensive Guide all about Small Businesses.** Go to this link to access https://nicholalett.lpages.co/small-business-mastery/

Introduction

Passive Income

PASSIVE INCOME, IN the simplest of terms, is the income that comes regularly and periodically to the recipient with minimal effort. For example, if you are renting a room in your house, you'll receive rent each month. You're earning money without actively working for it. Therefore, this income is a passive income.

That's not the only way to earn passive income, however. Other sources that can generate passive income include stocks, lottery wins, capital gains, online work, and dozens of other income paths and venues. These categories are widely accepted as an integral part of passive income even though the IRS only focuses on rental incomes when taking passive income into account. In addition, the IRS also includes the total income from the businesses in which the recipient is not materialistically participating in as well.

What does material participation mean?

If you're an investor who invests in some type of business, but does not participate in daily operations of that business, you are not considered to be engaging in material participation. You will still get a share of the profits from whatever the business earns, but you're not in an office making day-to-day operations decisions, thus you aren't actively participating. Ta-da, passive income!

Why is this considered passive income? This type of earning is passive income because the investor isn't participating in the running of the business. However, if the investor begins to manage the company affairs, the income earned by the investor could turn into active income. It's all about how much and where you decide to participate.

Multiple Streams Income Streams

There are many ways to create a passive income that will supplement your regular salary. If you make enough money, you won't have to worry about covering any new expenses you might incur, and you can also build a substantial savings. The only drawback is the potential need to keep your 9 to 5 job for steady income. If you make a nice living with your passive income and you can quit your day job, that's great. On the other hand, if your side income doesn't cover all your expenses, you should consider multiple income streams. Multiple income streams allow you to generate money from different sources. For example, one person might work as a virtual assistant and music reviewer. So, multiple checks are received at the end of every pay cycle.

Starting a Home Business

The benefits of starting a home business are numerous, but there are a few big pluses that definitely warrant a mention.

- **You are your own boss:**

    With a home business, you don't have to work for someone to make a living. In a day-to-day job, you might work for a demanding boss that makes your life miserable. You may also want more control of what you're doing. By being your own boss, you make your own rules.

- **A newfound passion for what you do:**

  People often lack the passion for what they do for a living and don't feel motivated to work. With a home business, the amount of money you earn depends on how much work you do. If you don't work, you don't get paid. How's that for motivation?

- **Lower taxes:**

  Even though the tax laws vary, every region imposes certain taxes on 9 to 5 jobs. In general, if you're running your own business, the taxes are considerably lower compared to taxes implemented on corporations.

- **No office politics:**

  Have you ever walked into a room and everyone stops talking? Do you hate working with that lady that stabs everyone in the back to get a management position? These scenarios and others happen to people every day. What's the answer to this? Start your own business. You choose who you want to work with, if anyone, and can leave all the backstabbing, office politicking, troublemakers behind.

- **Vacation:**

  The average vacation time for an employee with one year vested in a company is two weeks. If you have a family, most of your vacation time might be spent at the doctor's office, at home taking care of sick children, or taking a mental break away from work. With a home business, any day can be a vacation. You set your own hours and decide when you want to work.

- **Portability:**

Most people spend their lives stuck in traffic. Who wants to sit in a car all day? I don't, and I'm sure you don't either. Portability is a major advantage of owning your own business. If you have a laptop, phone, and a good WIFI connection, you can work just about anywhere. I'll take the beach over a loud, annoying office any day.

- **Greatly reduced risk of being fired:**

When you work for a company, there's always a risk of being fired or laid off. Unfortunately, this is the norm for corporations faced with the tough decision to cut costs and reduce spending. You may think your company can't survive without you, but it can and will. A home business will save you the headache and worry of seeing a pink slip sitting on your desk. In addition, since most people who own home businesses have more than one revenue source, you won't lose your entire income if a business venture doesn't work out.

Now that we know the benefits, let's focus on some home business opportunities and passive income jobs that can give you more money in your pocket.

Chapter 1
Get Paid Writing Song Reviews

IN THIS DIGITAL world, brands are marketing their products online. This not only applies to electronics and other gadgets, but also songs, movies, and a plethora of other platforms. If you're a music lover, this might be something right up your alley. Artists try to spread the word about new music on social media, as well as gathering good reviews so that the people who read those reviews will be attracted to their music.

How do these artists find these reviewers and, more importantly, how do these reviewers get paid?

A site that can help you get started is Slice the pie. Slice the pie is a company that pays you for every review you write. The money you earn can be anywhere from $0.01 to $0.05 per review. This may not sound like a lot, but over time, this money can add up. You can also get additional bonuses as well for your review. Once your balance reaches a minimum of $10, payments are sent to you via PayPal.

Musicxray is another site that lets you listen to music and pays you for it as well. Here is how it works:

The website provides a song that you listen to. You get paid $0.10 for every song. You must, however, listen to at least 30 seconds of the song to get paid. If you like certain songs, you can save your preferred genres and artists in your profile. Musicxray will collect music that matches your preferences and send you the songs to listen to. Payments are distributed through PayPal when your account reaches a minimum of $20.

If this sounds like something you'd like to do to make extra cash, there are minimal requirements for it. All you need is a computer and internet connection. To better listen to the music, you may want to invest in a good pair of headphones or a set of speakers. And most important, you need a PayPal account to receive all the money you rake in.

Chapter 2

Organize Festivals and Collect Money from Vendors

ORGANIZING FESTIVALS IS another cool way to earn a steady passive income. With the amount of work that it takes to plan events, this can easily turn into a home business. Festival themes can range from car shows, craft expos, or wedding planning events. If you're organizing a festival, there will be a lot of vendors that are interested in selling their products. You can ask these vendors to pay money to display and sell their products at your festival. The benefit is that you don't need to do any work for it. You can simply give each vendor a spot where they can sell whatever they wish to sell. If you need something more upscale, you can provide indoor product displays as well. Of course, you can charge higher rent for those.

When organizing your festival, the goal is to sell tickets and booth space. To start, you can sell tickets in advance. This allows you to earn more money, create publicity, and get a lot of attention. One way to make advance ticket sales attractive is to offer buyer discounts on advance purchases and bulk ticket deals. To manage ticket sales and your event, it's best to create a website and PayPal account to collect money. Sites like weebly.com and eventbrite.com are good resources.

Organizing festivals will require an investment. You need to find a venue that can accommodate your event. This may require a deposit and other fees. If you plan to serve alcohol or food, most states require a license. You may also need clearance for the use of speakers, fireworks, and other devices. Therefore, make sure you know the city ordinances in your area before organizing the festival.

Lastly, there are costs associated with printing tickets, setting up a website, and marketing your event. The money can add up, but there's a good chance that you'll make a return on your investment.

Chapter 3
Investing in Stocks

THE STOCK MARKET is a booming business in today's world. However, most people are either unaware of how the stock system works or have a negative perception about it. Since stocks are a popular and proven way to earn money, let's discuss the basics.

What are stocks?

Stocks basically represent your portion of ownership in a company. If a company is earning and making a profit, you will get a share of those profits based on the number of stocks (shares) you have in the company. Additionally, these stocks can be bought or sold as per the wishes of the owner.

When companies need funds for continuing their operations, they issue shares of the company to the public. This is called the Initial Public Offering (IPO). The cost of the shares depends on the worth of the company.

Since there are fluctuations in the market and company performance, stock prices vary. Therefore, people are scared to buy stocks since they think that it can mean a big loss for them.

How does the stock market work?

The stock market is a science. When a company issues stocks, the stocks are traded on stock exchanges such as the New York Stock Exchange (NYSE). Traders and investors gather here to buy and sell stocks of various companies. The prices of the stocks depend on how good a company is performing.

It is hard to predict the price of a stock beforehand as well as tell which stock will rise and which stock will fall. As time progresses, the stocks in general rise gradually. Therefore, the investors buy stocks in various sectors so that it can give them gradual profits over time.

Wondering how you're going to make money with stocks?

Making money with stocks is not complicated. To start, you need stocks that pay dividends to the stockholders, or you can buy stocks that will increase in value over time. Good sites for first time investors are:

- Merrill Edge
- TD Ameritrade
- Motif

You do not need a huge investment to open an account with a brokerage firm; however, you may be required to pay subscription fees and have a minimum account balance. Once your account is set up, you can buy stocks for even a few dollars.

Chapter 4
Mystery Shopping

MYSTERY SHOPPING IS a comparatively unknown way of making money passively. Most people don't know what it means, even if its name gives out a slight hint. A mystery shopper gets paid money or some other incentive to visit a retail outlet, buy products, and check the customer experience during the whole process. The exact specifics can differ from situation to situation, however, the basic principle behind the activity is the same.

Why do companies pay you to shop?

Companies often want to ensure that their customers get complete customer satisfaction. There's a lot of competition out there.

To ensure customers are getting the best possible treatment in stores, companies require mystery shoppers to fill out a checklist after a store visit. Some questions may include:

- Are customers greeted every time they walk into the store?
- Are customers greeted with a smile?
- What's the average customer wait time during checkout?
- Is the store clean?
- Are there any broken fixtures or other hazards?
- Are the restrooms clean?
- Are the aisles clear?

Mystery Shopping Agencies

Mystery shopping agencies hire people to do the mystery shopping for them. The ideal candidates can visit several stores and record their customer experience. Some agencies train shoppers to understand how they should score establishments. Once trained, shoppers enter stores and pretend to be customers. When the store evaluation is complete, the mystery shopper is paid for the visit and reimbursed for the products purchased.

If you want to earn decent money doing mystery shopping, you'll need to sign up with several mystery shopping agencies. Since this is an easy way to make money, there will be quite a few applicants competing for mystery shopping jobs. To start, join agencies that are members of reputable mystery shopping associations, such as the Mystery Shoppers Coalition, and the Mystery Shopping Providers Association. Joining a well-known agency reduces your change of running into a fraudulent company that could potentially scam you out of money. That's why it's important to do your research.

To become a mystery shopper, you'll need a computer with an internet connection. This is needed to submit completed questionnaires and surveys. In some cases, you may also be required to upload photos.

Reliable transportation is a major requirement. You need a way to get to and from all the retail establishments you visit. Most agencies don't reimburse you for transportation expenses, so it's important to keep some extra gas money handy.

Mystery shopping assignments can range anywhere from local boutiques to high-end restaurants, so you need to dress the part. A simple pair of jeans and a nice shirt will do, but be prepared to put on that nice dress or fancy blazer when visiting upscale places.

For quick notes and photographs, you'll need some type of mobile device. A smartphone or iPad will work well. If you see anything that would be helpful or notable, snap a quick pic and include it in your report. Your attention to detail and willingness to go above and beyond as a mystery shopper will likely snag you additional experiences in the future.

Mystery shopping is one of the best outlets for people who love to shop and who want to earn a little extra money doing so. If this seems like something you'd be interested in, get moving and get shopping!

Chapter 5

Create a Transportation Service for the Elderly

CREATING A TRANSPORTATION service for the elderly is an innovative way to start a home business. While there are a lot of companies that provide transportation services, there are few companies, if any exist in your area, which focus their services especially on the elderly.

Elderly people sometimes have difficulty traveling on public transportation and may require additional assistance. Therefore, providing transportation services for the elderly may be in high demand and pay big dividends, but it will also be a service to the community on your part.

This home business venture requires a decent investment in licensing and maintaining comfortable, adequate, and reliable transportation. However, the returns in this type of passive income job are huge.

Here are a few things that you need:

A Good business name: Just stating the obvious, but a name is something that you need for any business. Think of something catchy and not too cliché like, "Driving Miss Daisy Transportation" (this name is taken already, but you get the picture).

A business License: To operate your business legally, you'll need to get a business license according to state requirements.

Two of the most common licenses are sole proprietorships or limited liability companies (LLC).

A sole proprietorship doesn't include demarcation of personal and professional assets; therefore, you oversee all profits and debts. However, LLC business owners are not personally responsible for company debts and do not incur double taxation. Personal and business assets are separate. Business owners are also protected against company lawsuits.

If you're still undecided, it's important to speak to an attorney or accountant before proceeding with your business plans.

Business equipment: To manage your company, you must have a computer system with a good internet connection. You'll also need software. Most computers come with trial software that will allow you to maintain expenses, client information, and schedules. When the trial period is over, be sure to factor in monthly or yearly software license fees into your business expenses. Another important piece of equipment is a smartphone. This is essential because clients need a way to contact you to schedule rides. To avoid being late for an appointment because you were lost, you also need a GPS device. However, most smartphones have GPS applications. If not, Google Maps is a free application that you can download to get you from point A to point B without any issues.

Websites: Websites are good tools for new businesses. In this age of technology, owning a website is equivalent to having a cell phone number. So, what better way to promote your business than to have a website. If you're not very tech savvy, that's okay. There are plenty of sites that make the process of building a website easy. Godaddy.com is a great service that offers domain names, website building, and hosting services.

A valid driver's license: Since this is a business where the human risk factor is involved, you'll need a valid license with a clean driving record. To get more specifics, check your local and state agencies.

Reliable Transportation: If you're opening a transportation service, you'll obviously need reliable transportation. Further, as the transportation service focuses on the elderly, your car must be in good condition. You can start with one car and increase the number as the business grows.

Advertising: To make your business known in the community, you need to advertise. Business cards are a great way to promote your company. The good news is that you don't have to break the bank to get personalized cards. Companies like vistaprint.com offer printed business cards for as low as $16. They also print flyers and offer to mail your marketing material to potential customers. You can target a mail campaign to places where the elderly frequent or where their family members are likely to seek assistance with the elderly in their care.

Important Tips

If you're hiring drivers, it's important to submit the necessary tax forms (based on your area) and confirm that each driver has a clean driving record. You should verify all documents provided by potential drivers and check all references before hiring.

It's very important to check all governing agencies in your area regarding transportation services. Some areas only allow the pickup of customers from specified locations such as taxi stands.

In addition, do your research when it comes to charging your clients for their transportation as most will want you to wait while they do their shopping, doctor's appointments, etc. This additional time must be figured into your cost because it may minimize the number of clients you can handle in one day.

Lastly, always keep a first aid kit in all vehicles that you use. It's also helpful to take a course in CPR in case of an emergency.

If you love elderly people and enjoy providing lucrative services for those in need, creating your own transportation service for the elderly is precisely the sort of business you need to get into. With a little bit of ingenuity, technical know-how, and a passion for driving, you can create a revenue stream that will provide you with a steady source of income for as long as you choose to stay in the business. So what are you waiting for? Get started!

Chapter 6

Laundry Service

NOBODY LIKES THE time-consuming task of doing laundry. Using a laundry service is a lot better than wasting your time manually doing the chore. You can save a lot of time and effort by using a reliable laundry service, and therefore, your need to do the laundry is taken care of.

There are a lot of laundry services that are coming on the scene to take care of people's laundry needs. In order to provide the best service, the perks that laundry services offer to people have continuously been increasing to keep up with the competition. They try to minimize the time and effort on the client's part.

Therefore, the new and unexplored venture that has risen out of this market is picking up the laundry from the houses of people and doing their laundry for them. Anyone can do this and it gives you decent money.

One such website is Laundry Care. At Laundry Care, you can register yourself and provide laundry services to the people who are in your area. These services can be small scale or large commercial scale, depending on your preference.

Laundry Care is an innovative work-from-home opportunity where you can spend a lot of time with your family as well. Plus, there is not much labor on your part, your laundry machine is going to do all the hard work while you sit down and count the money.

If you're working for Laundry Care, you have to simply pick up the laundry, do the laundry, and return it within a certain time. It's as simple as that.

The pickup time of the laundry will depend on the client's preferred day and time. Some tips that require nothing but diligence on your part include being punctual and being polite at pickup. It's common sense, but it will greatly help long term by establishing a good relationship with clients.

Next, you'll need to wash the laundry. Follow by drying, folding, or hanging the laundry the client prefers. You should make sure that you take note of the client's preferences when you pick up the laundry and double check any care tips provided in the clothing itself. Laundry done right will lead to greater customer satisfaction and greater retention.

You're supposed to get back to the client and return the clean laundry within a 24-hour timeframe. This is a reasonable time to do the laundry and a busy client will definitely appreciate the quick turnaround.

There are additional services that you could include with the laundry service. These services can be ironing the clothes or dry cleaning them. Obviously, you'll be paid an additional amount depending upon the service.

Picking up laundry from people's homes is a very innovative and good way to earn some money. It's a flexible setup and you are your own boss. There is also minimal risk involved in this business. Further, the startup cost is not very much either. After all, how much does a washing machine cost? The chances are high that you already have one.

If you're working for a laundry service like Laundry Care, they're going to handle all the hard work for you. They take care of the client sign-ups and handle all the marketing aspects of the business. You don't have to worry about spreading the word because they will have already taken care of that.

Further, you can choose the area in which you wish to work. When clients who are in your area sign up for a laundry service, you're free to decide if you want to do their laundry or not. Everything is entirely up to you. Not only that, the company takes care of billing as well.

The money paid out is very decent too. Since you choose your clients, your earnings totally depend on the number of clients you have and the hours you want to work. On an average, you can earn around $250 in 12 hours through this business.

To start a business through Laundry Care, you need to buy their starter kit. This kit costs $95 and contains some of the essential supplies that you need in your venture. The package is sold at no-profit according to the website. It includes:

- Nylon laundry bags
- Processing bags
- Tags
- Garment covers
- 250 business cards

- 50 cards for racks
- 50 brochures
- A guide
- A location-based web page

Once you've signed up, the team at Laundry Care will create advertisements specific to your area. Your local web page will be optimized as well so that you can score higher in the search results. They will also give you access to their library, which contains a digital database of flyers that you can download and print out for yourself.

When you're operating the business on an ongoing basis, there are no running costs that you need to pay. In case any supply runs out, you can order them via the company. Of course, you'll need to buy additional detergent and fabric softener when you need them.

You are paid $20 for every regular garment bag you handle. For extra-large bags, $40 is paid out. Additional services like ironing, dry cleaning, or 24-hour rush, will give you extra compensation.

If you're dedicating around 15 hours per week, you can easily make $300. If you increase your commitment to 15-35 hours, expect around $500-700 each week.

That's great money, especially for a part time gig. A little dedication coupled with an ability to wash and fold will enable you to keep the piggy bank happy. If laundry is your go-to chore, this is one business opportunity that you can't afford to miss out on. Get to folding!

Chapter 7
Online Researcher

ONLINE RESEARCH IS one field that is an attractive opportunity for someone who wants to earn good money from a passive income job. There are a lot of organizations that are looking for people to work for them by doing research on a variety of topics. These organizations range from legal firms to medical institutions. It's not just these institutions, but even college students hire online researchers for their online thesis and research materials. If you enjoy doing the "legwork" by gathering relevant data for a client, this might be an opportunity that is right for you.

So, how do you choose which industry or topics to offer research on? Well, the research field that you choose depends on your experience. If you're in the legal field, a legal research job will benefit you. Medical professionals like CNAs, NPs, or RNs might choose medical research assignments because they will already have a good knowledge base to start with. Don't have any expert certifications? Don't stress. There are many research jobs that require no prior experience in the fields you'll be researching so long as you have an idea on how to conduct a good internet search.

Finding the jobs you seek might be daunting, but a great place to start meeting clients is through well-known job boards where clients post seeking candidates just like you.

Online job boards regularly publish jobs in various sectors. You can visit these job boards, create a profile, and find research positions. These boards have countless services that will assist you in your job search. Here are some suggestions:

Indeed.com: Indeed is a popular job search board where can find you countless work-from-home job opportunities. You'll find complete company profiles along with the job description. However, you should keep in mind that many job postings on this website are scams as well. You should never take a job that asks you for money, or that requires you to transfer money into some other account. To find online research job opportunities, use the keywords "work at home" or "internet research."

Flexjobs: Flexjobs focuses on flexible working arrangements. An important thing to note about Flexjobs is that there is a small fee to use their services. However, the huge advantage of Flexjobs is that the jobs are screened and completely verified. Therefore, you can apply without fear of being scammed. In the end, Flexjobs provides a comfort and ease of application that is definitely worth the small fee associated.

Upwork: Upwork is one of the most popular freelance job sites in the world. All you must do is register for a free account and you're good to go. Simply search for the right research job and you'll find countless results. However, there are a limited number of jobs you can apply for (30 jobs per month). If you want to apply for more, you can pay for premium services. Further, each time you work for a client, 20% is deducted as the UpWork fee.

All in all, these job boards are just tools to get you started. Once you're able to establish consistent clients with regular work, you may choose to switch to a direct pay method with them and simply wait for your assignments like any other work opportunity.

Expert Advice for Cash

Another way to integrate online research into cash is to answer questions on paid forums. This is basically a Q&A session for people who are seeking advice or informed research on a topic but are unable to find that information themselves or want to verify the research they have already conducted with an expert in the field.

A couple of websites worth exploring are:

Wonder is a site that hires people to research information. To use this service, students and professionals must submit their technical and non-technical questions on the website. Once questions are submitted, freelancers perform research and find solutions. For example, a researcher could research the number of celebrities that live in New York City.

Just Answer: This website hires experts to provide solutions to questions. The money that you earn from this source will depend on the number of hours per week that you put in for the website and the field in which you are an expert. Generally, it requires a certificate or a degree that proves that you are an expert in the field that you claim to have knowledge about.

Experts123: In this website, you can write articles as well as answer the popular questions for money. The amount of money that you receive will depend on the number of views that your answers or articles are generating.

Your pay depends on the time that it will take to answer questions, as well as the complexity of the question. Researchers who are at the top of their field can earn around $35 per hour. This can easily give them $2000 per month as a passive income. The website pays every two weeks through PayPal.

Virtual Research Assistants

Virtual research assistants, often just shortened to virtual assistants on job boards, are freelancers who help clients with a variety of tasks on the internet, often on a consistent basis. Unlike many regular personal assistants, majority of your research will revolve around things like the best flight deals, hotels that meet client expectations, organizing a list of appropriate venues for a client's event, and other tasks that require research and legwork that a busy client may not have time for.

There are several advantages to being a virtual assistant over a regular personal assistant, namely that you aren't stuck working for any one client to secure your job and that you can have more than one client at a time. You are free to find your own clients through job boards, freelancing sites, and other job service sites that may be specific to your field of expertise.

The client may have you working with a team of people for an assignment, so make sure to check the parameters of the assignment before you agree to work it. If you're working with a team, you might work together with content writers, graphic designers, internet marketers, etc. and research material on the internet for them to use.

There are very few limits on what a client might ask you to research, market trends, business analysis, hotel accommodations, flight information, or a great place to eat for lunch, the sky is the limit.

Decided you want to try being an online researcher? Here are the things that you need to get started:

- **An online connection:** This might seem to go without saying, but a consistent internet connection will help you stay connected with clients and allow you to research reliably.

- **Spreadsheets:** Spreadsheets will help you keep track of your research and allow you to manage your findings in an organized way. Google offers a free version called Sheets that is very effective.

- **Attention to detail:** As a researcher, making sure you get the details right is key. If you're a big-picture person who misses out on those key details, this may not be the job for you. If you love getting into the nitty gritty details, this is right up your alley and perfect for you.

If research is your passion, being an online research guru is a great passive way to earn money. Whether you decide to become a personal assistant or an independent researcher for a Q&A service, you'll love answering the questions the world throws at you in the varied fields associated with online research.

Chapter 8
Start a Dog Walking Business

IF YOU, LIKE many pet lovers the world over, are used to walking the dog and find it to be one of the most enjoyable hours of the day, why not turn your enjoyment into a side business? Dogs are one of the most loved pets on the planet and owners spend an average of $3000 per dog per year, meaning a lot of money is dropped every day on everyone's favorite animal daily. Cashing in on this multi-million dollar industry should be a piece of cake, and it is.

People are busier than ever and these hectic schedules often prevent owners from giving their dogs much needed daily exercise and/or the right number of potty breaks throughout the day. To help dog owners, more and more people are hiring dog walkers. That's where you step in.

Dog walking is one of the most lucrative ventures to engage in. Since you can service several different clients at one time, this ensures that you are making an average of $20 per hour while you're working. What could be better than making money and hanging out with your favorite furry friends? If you love dogs and want to make some extra cash, a dog walking business might be a good fit for you. The best part is that it requires little investment on your part. Sound good? This business is just a short walk away.

If you have your own furry companion, you're probably familiar with a walking routine. Whether you're walking the dog for a short jaunt so it can go to the bathroom or walking a loop to make sure your dog gets at least 30 minutes of semi-vigorous exercise, you know that walking your animal is key to making your companion healthy and happy. People who hire dog walkers want the same thing for their own pets.

The two key traits you'll need to be a good dog walker are:

- A love for animals that enables you to interact with a wide variety of dogs with varying temperaments and, more importantly, the ability to judge, anticipate, and predict their needs while they are under your care.

- The ability to take dogs out for walks, often several hours out of the day, multiple days a week. While you might not have to be in Olympic running shape, you'll need to be able to at least walk and be on your feet several hours out of the day.

If you're a dog owner, you're probably familiar with these traits and possess them already. However, there are some differences between how you would treat your personal pet and how your day will look when you become a professional dog walker as well as some differences on how you will go about becoming a professional in your field.

Let's start from the beginning and find out what you need before you begin accepting clients.

A Business License: Most cities do not have specific licenses needed to operate a dog walking business, however, they will most likely require you to have a general business license. Depending on the city, you can either file this form online or in person at your local courthouse. The cost ranges state-to-state, from $50 to $200 depending on the location.

A Liability Fund: Since dog owners are entrusting you with their animals, you are liable for what happens to their dogs when in your care. If you are transporting the animals in your vehicle, make sure you have insurance which will cover the cost of medical care should you be unfortunate enough to get into an accident with the dogs. Furthermore, it wouldn't hurt to keep an emergency fund set aside in case Fifi and Tony decide to get into a scuffle at the dog park while on your watch. Having that extra level of protection will allow you to handle potentially highly stressful situations that occur with animals and face it with professionalism.

Pricing and Services: Generally, the services of dog walking are offered in time blocks like 15 minutes, half hour, 45 minutes, etc. You have the option to walk a single dog or multiple dogs from the same apartment complex or street. There are additional services that can be offered as well, such as obedience training, pet hostel, pet sitting, etc. The pricing of such services differs highly from locality to locality. In order to find out what the price is in your area, you need to check out the competitors and the prices that they're offering and advertise accordingly.

Liability & Paperwork: This might go without saying for most, but it is definitely important enough to mention. Having clients sign some sort of waver or limited liability contract before accepting animals in your care will enable you to ensure that if something beyond your power should happen, you will only assume limited liability and they can't turn around and make large legal claims against you to effectively kill your business. Check out sites like Legal Zoom for templates or, if you are more comfortable with handing the legal stuff over to a professional, consulting a lawyer who specializes in contracts isn't a bad idea.

Contracts: Before you start working with a new client, you should make sure that you have a contract with the client that is duly signed by you and the client. This client should clearly state the relationship present between the client, you, and the pet. In this contract, you should mention all the necessary clauses about the services you are offering to the client, the payment the client is making to you for those services, the cancellation policies, damages policies, and the scenarios of any emergency health situations. This is pretty basic across most service-based businesses and, again, Legal Zoom will most likely have templates for you and contract lawyers will have you squared away in a fairly limited time. Last but not least, make sure the contract is signed before you start working with a client. Retroactively signing paperwork looks unprofessional and it exposes you to liability or misunderstanding.

Advertising Materials: Setting up a website that advertises your services and having printed material ready to drop off at grooming salons, local hangouts, or interested clients you happen on at the dog park, will enable you to gain clients quickly. Platforms like Weebly, WordPress, GoDaddy, and Blogger have very low cost options for new business owners. Website domains can be bought for as little as $10 for a .com site. If you're a social media guru, set up your own page or profile on your site of choice and connect it to the lovely webpage you just bought. It will increase traffic to your site and get your business some additional attention. Free online advertising platforms like Craigslist, Facebook pages, and the likes are a great place to start throwing your name in the ring if you're in need of ideas.

Printed materials might have you cringing at your lack of graphic art skills, but no worries. Many printing services have their own design software that is easy-to-use and other free software like Canva, has drag and drop features that make even the most novice people into experts. If you use a third-party software, simply download your design and then upload it to the printing service. Most places like Vista Print have professionals that will adjust your template for the print and show you a mock up to approve before the final printing. Don't just stop at a pamphlet, print up a couple of t-shirts so that you can advertise wherever you go.

So you've got your business license, you have your marketing materials, and you either have your insurance up-to-snuff or a little nest egg set to the side. You are now ready to start collecting your clients. What does your day as a dog walker consist of? What do you need to get you through that day? Here is a snapshot.

You'll wake up and look at the schedule for today. You have clients scheduled at various intervals throughout the day with a couple of hours break in between for you to rest and grab some lunch. You don your most comfortable pair of sneakers, weather appropriate clothing, treats for the dogs, portable water bowl, and small bags for waste disposal. (The latter is very important because in most areas you can and will be fined if you fail to pick up after the dogs you're walking.)

Afterwards, you'll be ready to go about your schedule. Time management is very important here. You want to give yourself time to accomplish what you have promised and, most importantly, be on time for pickup and drop off. Some of your clients may be waiting for you to come retrieve their dogs from their homes before they go to work or waiting for you at a drop off location so they can get their own to-do lists finished. Whether your client is dropping off their pup or you're picking them up, Punctuality will make you a winner to them, we promise.

How many dogs should you schedule at one time? It really depends on you and how many animals you can handle. Dog walkers we interviewed said that the numbers of dogs they walk can range anywhere from two to ten dogs, depending on the size of the animals and the schedule, and that most animals were repeat customers, i.e. Fifi gets walked every day, Monday through Friday, at 1PM before Mom and Dad get home from work. Once you get a feel of how many you can handle and what sorts of breeds of dogs you'll be walking, you'll have a more accurate picture of what you can pencil in.

A key ingredient to having a successful trip out every time is to have good record keeping skills. Every dog you walk should have a client sheet to go along with it that enables you to have all the crucial information about the dog all in one place. You can type this up in any document creation program and print it out to use over and over again.

Things to include in your doggie snapshot:

- **A picture & description of the dog.** You might think you'll remember every furry face, but if you have six terriers, it will be understandable if you mistake Daisy for Marco. Having a picture will help you keep everyone straight.

- **Client contact information.** This information should include the home address, home & cell phone numbers, as well as an emergency contact number.

- **Vaccination dates as applicable by law.** Check what vaccinations are mandatory for dog owners to carry and make sure you have witnessed some sort of documentation that demonstrate your client possesses it. Most of the time Rabies is the minimum requirement, but all the mandatory vaccines should be available by consulting your local vet or government website.

- **Medications or conditions.** Make sure the owners disclose any sort of medical conditions their animal may have, even if they don't seem applicable to the hour or two you are with them. If something should happen, you might need to disclose that information to your vet in the case of an emergency.

- **Veterinarian information.** In addition to any medications or conditions the dog may have, you should include their chosen vet or vet facility where they're seen. This is a just-in-case bit of information that may one day come in handy.

The rest of your day will largely be spent outdoors on trails, walking paths, dog paths, and other dog-friendly hotspots in and around town. You'll make sure all your doggie clients get home, thanks to that handy-dandy doggie sheet, and you'll be ready to get home and get some rest.

Does the snapshot appeal to you? Then you might have just found your calling. If you weren't convinced enough by this point. Here are a few more perks to think about.

- You'll get to skip the gym membership thanks to all the walking you'll be doing.
- You'll get to spend time outdoors instead of in a cubicle.
- You can make your own schedule and schedule time off as you need.
- The potential to expand is limitless.
- The startup cost is low and therefore profit margins are high.

Now that you have all the things ready and in order, you are good to start your dog walking business. Get out there and enact a fun and delightfully fuzzy business venture and turn it into your dream come true.

Chapter 9
Independent Travel Consultant

IF YOU'RE LOOKING to make money, travel, and have one of the most exciting home business opportunities in the industry, you might want to consider becoming an independent travel consultant. Independent travel consultants work with customers to book flights, hotels, cruises, and destination activities for places all over the world. The best part? While experience may put you ahead of the learning curve, it isn't necessary to be successful in this work.

So how do you become an independent travel consultant? The paths to this are numerous, but there are a few commonalities that don't change. You'll need to have these things in place before you start collecting clients.

Connections. You might be scratching your head at this point and wondering h0w you go about forming business relationships with people and companies hundreds and, perhaps, thousands of miles away. Believe it or not, most reputable establishments will offer a commission rate to independent travel agents. Since these arrangements require very little from the companies in terms of upfront costs, the relationship works out very nicely for both parties.

Once you're established, agreeing to a goal referral number with the establishments can also gain things like increased bonuses, larger commissions, and freebies like free nights, meal vouchers, or airline points. Just make sure your contacts clearly outline the terms of your commission rate and you keep in contact with your point person to ensure there are no problems with your commission rates.

The majority of larger travel-based companies are vouched for via organizations like The American Society of Travel Agents, ASTA for short. These organizations protect the interests of the travel agents by providing reputable resources to travel consultants. Some even offer leads, a very helpful aspect for beginner travel consultants.

Independent travel consultants can join such an organization for a minimal yearly fee to gain access to their extensive databases, helpful publications, and a variety of other agent resources in order to be successful at the business, including discounts. Most even offer classes online if you need a place to start. ASTA offers one such a course for twenty-five dollars. The general overview is incredibly helpful for someone without any experience who may be unsure of where to start on their personal journey into this career. That isn't to say that you can't start your own database of connections from scratch. These organizations just offer to do the legwork for you.

Next question you must ask yourself: Host agency or no host agency? If running an entire business yourself seems a bit overwhelming, there are already branded hosting agencies that allow you to use their brand in order to gather clients and provide services to them. Most of these are niche, perhaps targeting cruise line customers or other specific travel need, and commissions vary agency to agency. 91% of independent travel consultants split their commissions with a hosting agency according to publications by NASTA and NACTA, another membership organization for the betterment of travel agents. So if niche markets appeal to you, this is probably a good fit.

If you decide a hosting agency is right for you, just make sure they fulfill their end of the bargain. They should offer you clear commission rates, accounting, agent support, and marketing benefits. If not, it might be a wasted commission split on your part.

Once you've decided on whether or not a hosting agency will be the right fit for you and you've made those connections to organizations that will help you provide your clients with destinations and services, it's time to invest your money. Now that everyone and their mother is available online, it should come as no surprise that you will need a website. This is where you decide on the look for your travel consultant work. Are you hip and modern? Classic and refined? Cruise-oriented? Destination oriented? What do you want to convey instantly to your potential clients?

Whatever identity you choose, make sure it is consistent throughout your website, business accouterment, and services offered.

You can do this by creating a website that offers a clear snapshot of who your business represents. To start, you can hire a website designer, a more expensive option but one that might be necessary for those of us who are not technologically savvy.

Working with a designer will enable you to get the look you want without having to put in a lot of work yourself. Just make sure to keep in communication with your designer so the final product turns out exactly what you want it to be. What does a designer run you? Usually these experts charge on average $59 per hour plus the cost of your URL, usually around $15 per year depending on where you buy the URL.

Another cheaper option is to create a website yourself through one of the numerous platforms that offer website templates. One such platform is Blogger, which is already Google integrated and easy to set up for SEO. Another platform that is quite user-friendly is Weebly. It offers a lot of template options, making the pickier website creator feel better about their numerous options. Your cost $.30 to $.69 per day, which is billed monthly and comes with all the interesting and necessary features like an integrated online checkout process and professional assessment tools. Again, the URL is separate but runs about the same as with a designer, $15 per site.

You'll need to keep a database of your contacts in an easy-to-access location. Google Sheets is excellent, and free, to use if you don't want to spring for Excel. If you want to purchase the Microsoft Suite, it runs about $200 before tax, but comes with Powerpoint, Word, and Excel, which can be useful for creating additional business documents. It is suggested that you also keep a physical copy of your contacts as well, just in case of technical failure. Printers and paper are extremely inexpensive these days, running as little as $20 for a printer and $10 for a huge stack of paper. If you don't want to deal with the headache of replacing cartridges and whatnot, many mailing services offer printing services as well for as little as $.05 per page printed.

So you have your website up, your contacts ready to go, and your memberships all set up. You are now ready to get out there and recruit some clients to start your next career as an independent travel consultant!

Chapter 10
Website Tester

WEBSITE TESTING IS a fairly new method of making passive income that can lead to a fairly simple and easy way to bring in extra income every month. If you like sharing your opinion, being a website tester is a great fit for you. There are many institutions that are interested in everyday users who can help them determine if user experience is a problem in their client websites. The best part? Getting into this particular way of making passive income is fairly simple.

So, what sort of things will you have to review? The design of the site, quality, and ease-of-use. If that sounds easy enough, let's find out how to get started.

You first need to determine whether you wish to start up your own web testing services company by creating a website and reaching out to companies who may need a web tester. If you're willing to work for a third-party, they will provide jobs from their own database of clients. Either is a viable option, but, to be honest, signing up for multiple third-party clients is probably the best way to go for a beginner because it takes the guess work out of making connections and establishing a good reputation with potential websites.

If you already have good connections and have a foothold in the computer science community, this may be a great way for you to expand and make an additional income on the side. Create a website, advertise your services, and reach out to your connections and you'll be able to provide feedback without any hassle. It's that simple.

If you're a beginner, as mentioned previously, you probably don't have the connections necessary to generate clients to make this a viable income stream. There are several third-party companies that payout freelance web testers consistently. Here are a few examples of websites you might want to sign up for:

UserTesting: Usually pays out between $10/$15 for 20 to 30 minutes of work. You sign up, take a brief test to make sure you are knowledgeable enough to do what they need, and then you can begin taking assignments.

Enroll: Register for the service and you'll begin receiving emails with assignments that vary in length. One user reportedly did a 1-minute project for a payout of .10, while others report that the average project takes between 15 and 20 minutes.

Startuplift: Sign up and companies will provide their sites and a set of questions they want answered. Write up your responses and send it in. You will be paid $5.00 per project.

TestingTime: This is one of the few companies that pays extremely well for the work you do. You can earn up to .50 per project, but they do expect you to do a bit more work than other website testing companies of their type. The assignments are discussed via Skype and can take up to 90 minutes to complete. You'll need a quiet space for these as you will be talking directly to clients via Skype. You'll also probably want to ditch the PJs since you'll be "face-to-face" at times.

These are just a few examples of sites that are available and represent some of the most popular of their type. It should be noted that no single website will provide enough work to make these assignments into a full time gig. Rather, if you're aiming to earn a higher payout, we suggest signing up for multiple sites to increase the amount of income earned as well as make sure you have several income streams coming at one time.

The equipment costs for this particular mode of passive income is very limited. All you need, in most cases, is an internet connection, laptop, cell phone, and/or other mobile device, as well as the ability to use services like Skype (in some cases.)

If you want the bells and whistles, you can also purchase a hands-free headset so you can more easily communicate, if you're making videos on website navigation. In addition, you can purchase Microsoft Word to write out your responses for those companies that prefer written feedback on their projects. Again, these are just optional add-ons and are not necessary to begin your journey into website testing. They are great tools, however, and might be an investment you make later on when you decide to continue doing these sorts of activities in the future.

Most of these companies pay out via PayPal, so if you're wanting to break into this mode of passive income, make sure you have that set up well ahead of time. You have the option with PayPal to link your account to your regular bank account and it is a relatively simple process, but one that can take several days to establish.

You can also order a PayPal debit card that will be linked directly to your PayPal balance. For those who wish to use this income as extra pocket money and don't plan on using PayPal for your other income streams, using your PayPal debit card will enable you to keep track of extra spending, making it another great option for those worried about separating out their "fun money" from their regular income.

All in all, website testing can be a semi-lucrative passive income stream that requires very little time and commitment to accomplish. It's definitely one of the better passive income opportunities out there.

Chapter 11

Sell Your T-Shirt Designs

HAVE A PASSION FOR fashion? This might be a great way for you to passively break into a multi-billion dollar a year industry. Spreadshirt is a company that allows you to open an online store featuring your unique designs on everything from t-shirts and hoodies to accessories, phone cases, and backpacks.

This is perfect for those who have digital artistic skills that they want to see other people wearing their art or people who have a way with words to get their messages out there. You just create your designs and then upload it in the Spreadshirt system and put it up in your store. The best part? There is no need to purchase the printable merchandise and print your designs, Spreadshirt does all that for you. You select the type of item you want to print on, upload your design and/or text, and then add it to your store page. The only thing left to do at that point is to watch the money roll in!

Don't have any design skills, but have a vision in mind? Try using a freelancing site like Fiverr to find an artist that will make your perfect design for as little as $5. It's definitely worth the initial investment since you'll be selling your creations on Spreadshirt for a commission of twice that per t-shirt sold.

Once a customer orders your design, Spreadshirt will print the item and mail it directly to the client. They also handle marketing and feature designs to sell more merchandise directly on their site in order to create more interest in their creative clients.

In return, on top of a design price that you set, you can earn up to 60% of the product price through their Affiliate and Volume commission structures. All around, the more you sell, the more you earn and Spreadshirt helps you get there, which is a definite plus over other printers.

You can also promote your store like any other online store via social media, online advertising, etc. Almost all promotional avenues are free or low cost, leaving you able to keep startup costs to a minimum.

Have we hooked you yet? Good. Here is what you need to get started:

- A stable internet connection and a laptop.
- A couple of starter designs.
- A few minutes a day to self-promote.

The very low cost of this way to make passive income makes it one of the easiest to maintain even if you have multiple revenue streams and/or other obligations.

Chapter 12
Transcribing Audio & Video

IF YOU ENJOY listening to other people's conversations, transcribing audio and video as an independent contractor may be the best home business opportunity for you. Transcriptionists work at home typing recorded conversations for a variety of industries for a set dollar amount per minute of recorded audio. These transcriptions can either be ordered as precise repetitions where every hiccup, pause, or false start is recorded, or as "polished" transcriptions that eliminate false starts, repetitions, and ambient sounds in order to create a smoother linear dialogue. The client will usually let you know what they expect well ahead of time and you'll know going in whether or not they want exact dialogue or not.

The types of recordings that you will encounter vary from client to client. Some clients will ask for medical transcriptions, transcriptions for sporting events, interviews with focus groups, podcasts, academic reviews, and subtitles for TV programs. The types of recordings are really unlimited because almost every walk of life needs audio transcribed into readable text, so be prepared for a wide variety of fields and genres.

When you type up these audio recordings, you can do so in a few different ways. Some third-party companies supply their own transcription programs that will easily mark the timestamp where you need to and allow you to type freely without worrying about purchasing any other software. Even if you decide to work independently, you can use Microsoft Word to type up your transcriptions. Just make sure that you have your formatting set up from the start so you won't have to wrestle with it later, i.e. in the middle of your next project!

If you really want to get professional, you can purchase a foot pedal with a USB connector that will enable you to pause audio or add a timestamp once it is setup for you. These range anywhere from 25 to several hundred dollars, depending on whether or not you want to add a specific transcription software or pedal style to your purchase. Average price for the pedals tend to be between $45 and $65.

You'll also need a good pair of headphones for transcription work because you'll be expected to pick up nuances in audio despite poor quality audio. Trust us when we say that some clients just can't seem to record their projects at a reasonable decibel no matter how hard they try! With a superior pair of headphones that are both comfortable, since you'll be using them for several hours at a time, and of good quality, you'll be able to tackle even the most difficult task without issue.

Breaking into transcription isn't nearly as difficult as some may think. There are many businesses out there who are desperate to find someone to transcribe their files, the key is finding them. If you're totally against working for a third-party company, you might be able to join a freelancing site and bid on projects and network with clients to establish a consistent stream of income. Again, this might work well for some, but for the large majority of people looking to make passive income, this idea may not necessarily appeal. The legwork, so to speak, will take up a lot of time and dealing with clients one-on-one can be a hassle.

Most choose to go through third-party sites similar to the ones we recommend for website testing since this enables all the legwork to be completed before you even begin the project. Websites like Rev.com or DailyTranscription.com will make you perform a test to measure your proficiency as a typist and how well you can hear and transcribe the audio correctly. These tests are usually unpaid and may take up to an hour of time, though most average much less at 20 minutes or so.

Once you pass, you'll be added to their database of active users and will be able to see the projects they have available. Most are first-come first-serve and will inform you upfront what you'll be paid for your project. Most sites will also list what the project's subject matter is along with a brief, usually 10 to 15 second, sample of the audio.

Pay for the projects is directly related to how long the audio file is as well as how quickly the client needs it translated. Third-party sites will do this calculation for you and will show you exactly how much you'll be making for the amount of work you'll be doing, a very convenient service for those who just want to log on and work.

Startup costs for being a transcriptionist are fairly minor since you can afford to go a little more inexpensively in the beginning without a huge penalty. You'll need a laptop with an internet connection, a pair of earphones, and possibly a document creating program, depending on the transcription services you offer or if the organization you're partnering with has a transcription program already set up.

Skills that you need are a fast typing speed, anything less than 60 WPM is probably going to slow you down too much to really accomplish what you need to within a reasonable time frame, and the ability to hear words from audio recordings without being able to look at a person's mouth. This won't be as much of an issue if you're doing only video transcription, depending on the project, but it is critical for accuracies sake in majority of the projects you'll come across.

What are the potential programs with transcription? Well, some of the types of transcription that you may enjoy may be seasonal. For example, if you enjoy working on academic transcriptions, you most likely will not be able to find them outside of the academic calendar or you may find much fewer of them during this time. Likewise, if you enjoy listening to baseball podcasts, these might not be available for transcription outside the season.

All in all, transcription is a fairly lucrative business opportunity that will enable you to make as little or as much as you need to. This is one of the few types of jobs on our list that you can reasonable hope to make a full time wage from the word "go," making it one of the most highly recommended avenues for freelancers everywhere.

Chapter 13
Online Tutor

IF YOU HAVE a love of learning and passing on knowledge, making some extra money through tutoring students online should be right up your alley. With the interconnectedness of the modern world, it's no wonder that people are able to learn online from anywhere in the world. Whether you're tutoring high school students in preparation for the SAT or helping Chinese students half a world away work on their English skills, it is possible to tutor and make a decent hourly wage by doing so.

Online tutoring is fairly self-explanatory. You'll be creating a lesson plan and then using it to help a student to better themselves in your preferred subject areas. For example, if you're teaching an English as a second language student, you would be tutoring a foreign language student in simple English lessons and testing and aiding their proficiencies in the English language.

Getting tutoring gigs is also fairly easy thanks to their pretty aggressive advertising on hiring websites like Indeed.com and Monster.com. Here's a list of websites users are finding the greatest success with and those which pay out on a regular basis:

Vipkid: This tutoring service specializes in immersive English teaching for Chinese learners, primarily school age children. They have preset lesson plans already set up for teachers and pay out bimonthly.

The Princeton Review: If you've been to college, you have probably heard of The Princeton Review and have seen the numerous supplemental study materials they churn out each year. This service better prepares high school students for college and helps them up their scores for the ACT & SAT. The great thing about tutoring or teaching part time for The Princeton Review is that you have the ability to tutor in your subject matter to English-speaking students.

You'll be playing to your strengths and be able to pass on your knowledge to the next generation while making upwards of $20 per hour doing so. Subject matters that are higher in demand, things like Chemistry for example, can pay even more than that at $35 an hour.

College Pirates: This is a tutoring service that specializes in tutoring college students in subject matters of your specialty, again, enabling you to work in your niche expertise. Unlike many similar online programs, this one doesn't require your Masters or PhD to tutor college students. It just requires "reasonable credentials." What that entails, it is hard to say, but most recommend having at least a bachelor's degree before applying. Tutors make up to $25 per hour.

These are just a few of the sites out there that are offering tutoring services. Like being a website tester, it isn't a bad idea to sign up for multiple websites in order to maximize your income potential.

The application process varies slightly from site to site, but the consistency seems to be to fill out the online application and offer your credentials in the form of a resume. From there, they will issue a test that usually involves a mock lesson, and then they will begin setting you up with clients. The skills required for these jobs is almost always a personable demeanor.

There are several technological concerns that are critical to be successful in these sorts of jobs.

First, you must have a internet connection with a minimum bandwidth and speed because you most likely will be running programs similar to Skype and must maintain a good connection to conduct your lesson properly. You may even want to make sure you're able to hardline into your internet to prevent any dips in the speeds thanks to multiple WIFI connectivity.

Secondly, you need to have a headset that allows you to communicate hands-free with your students. Springing for the higher end headsets will definitely aid you in being understood and in understanding your students as you move through your lessons.

Thirdly, you need a good laptop and camera. No one wants to look at a crummy image when they're paying for a service. If you don't enjoy pixilated, lagging images when you are watching Netflix, imagine how much more annoying it would be if you were trying to learn something from them.

Some additional aspects to consider would be professional attire. We're not saying you should go out and put on a suit and tie when you tutor, but not wearing pajamas will lend you more credence as an educator and will more likely lead to repeat customers. Throw on a collared shirt and brush your hair. It's as simple as that.

Last, but certainly not least, consider if you have a clean space to teach without interruptions. Students might consider you "cool" if you have your favorite band poster hanging above your bed while you're teaching, but it might not be their parent's favorite thing about you. Pick a clean, clutter-free space that has an ounce of quiet. Examples would include a rarely-used dining room table or even the living room.

If you enjoy passing on your knowledge to the next generation and like the idea of a stay-at-home job that pays well, becoming an online tutor is a passive income that is right up your alley. The flexibility in the hours and the minimum monetary investment really makes this one of the best avenues for passive incomes on our list. If teaching your favorite subject is something you love, put in your applications and sign up today so that you can take advantage of the untapped income that tutoring offers.

Chapter 14

Get Going!

PASSIVE INCOME AND home business opportunities are a very needed and a sought-after commodity in a world where a single active income and traditional job are not enough to fulfill the dreams of most people. Many compromise their needs and settle for what they can afford with their active income, but since you've come this far, you're clearly looking ahead. With the ideas that are mentioned in this book, you'll never need to settle for anything. These ideas require minimal startup cost and can be followed by anyone without any expertise in any field.

But of course, you should always tread with caution when you're starting a business. A business venture is like your own child. It's your own business. Therefore, how you run it is important. You should pay attention to what the customers feel about your services. If your customers like your services, they'll continue to use your service. No matter which opportunity you opt for, customer satisfaction is a must.

Further, while the passive income jobs and home business opportunities that we mentioned have little or no startup costs, there are some areas where you may need to spend. For example, if you're doing an online research job, you should have a good computer system with fast internet connectivity. If you're using an obsolete computer system that freezes after every 2 minutes, you will be wasting most of your time. Also, you might need to make Skype calls or online conferences during any of the work-from-home opportunities. That will require a good internet connection. If you do not have one, it's going to reflect badly on your professionalism. And you should always strive to give out your best.

This is not only limited to online businesses, but other businesses as well. For example, if you're in the laundry business, you're getting paid generously for the laundry that you're doing. Therefore, you should not shy away from using good quality products like detergents and softeners. If you don't spare some money in these investments and settle for the cheapest alternatives, the output will be poor and your clients might end up being disappointed with the services you offer. As a golden rule, remember that no businesses can survive with a bad relationship with their clients.

Thankfully, we've assembled the tools to provide a smooth transition from the thought of creating a business to generating an income. So long as you have a plan, do your best to provide excellent customer service, and fulfill your promises, you will have no worries when it comes to maintaining a stellar business reputation. Additionally, you'll see your income streams swell with increasing profits.

The benefits of having a passive income source and home business are numerous and, with dedication, they can fulfill avenues that you haven't even considered yet. Passive income jobs can be done side by side with regular jobs or multiply enough to generate full income potential and lead to successful home businesses. In most cases, you're your own boss and you work on your own terms, so these opportunities can be a great way to empower yourself. Whether you're coming home from a regular 9 to 5 or trying to build a portfolio of business ventures that puts you firmly in the driver's seat, starting your own business or generating passive income is never a bad idea.

Have a friend you're dying to work with? You can team up and complete jobs in half the time. Unlike most other active income jobs, you get to decide who works with you. What else could you ask for?

Anyone can create income with the ideas described in this book. It's just that simple. These jobs don't require you to put in a lot of hours, and they don't require a lot of monetary investment. Try one of them out or several of them so you can find exactly the right fit that allows you to make money without struggling to find interest in what you're doing. Pursue your passions. Try something new. Most importantly, have fun!

One Last Thing...

If you enjoyed this book or found it useful I'd be very grateful if you'd post a short review on Amazon. Your support really does make a difference and I read all the reviews personally, so I can get your feedback and make this book even better.

Also, don't forget to download the free gift from me to you: Go to this link to instant access: https://nicholalett.lpages.co/small-business-mastery/

Thanks again for your support!

www.ingramcontent.com/pod-product-compliance
Lightning Source LLC
Chambersburg PA
CBHW030035230526
45472CB00002B/517